£1-50

Contents

Paper in practice	8
Growing paper	10
From tree to timber	12
From wood to pulp	14
From pulp to paper	16
Coating and cutting	18
Looking at paper	20
Make your own paper	22
Paper projects	24
Paper past and present	26
Glossary	28
Index	29

Paper in practice

All around us there are things made of the amazing material called paper, from soft tissues to strong cardboard boxes. Paper can be used in so many ways because it has lots of different properties. Why do you think it has been chosen to make all the things shown here?

And did you know that all paper, whatever it is made into, begins as a living plant?

Growing paper

All paper is made from plant fibres. These are tiny tubes of cellulose that make up a plant's stem or leaves. Nowadays most fibres for paper come from trees specially grown for papermaking. These trees grow in huge forests, usually in cool parts of the world.

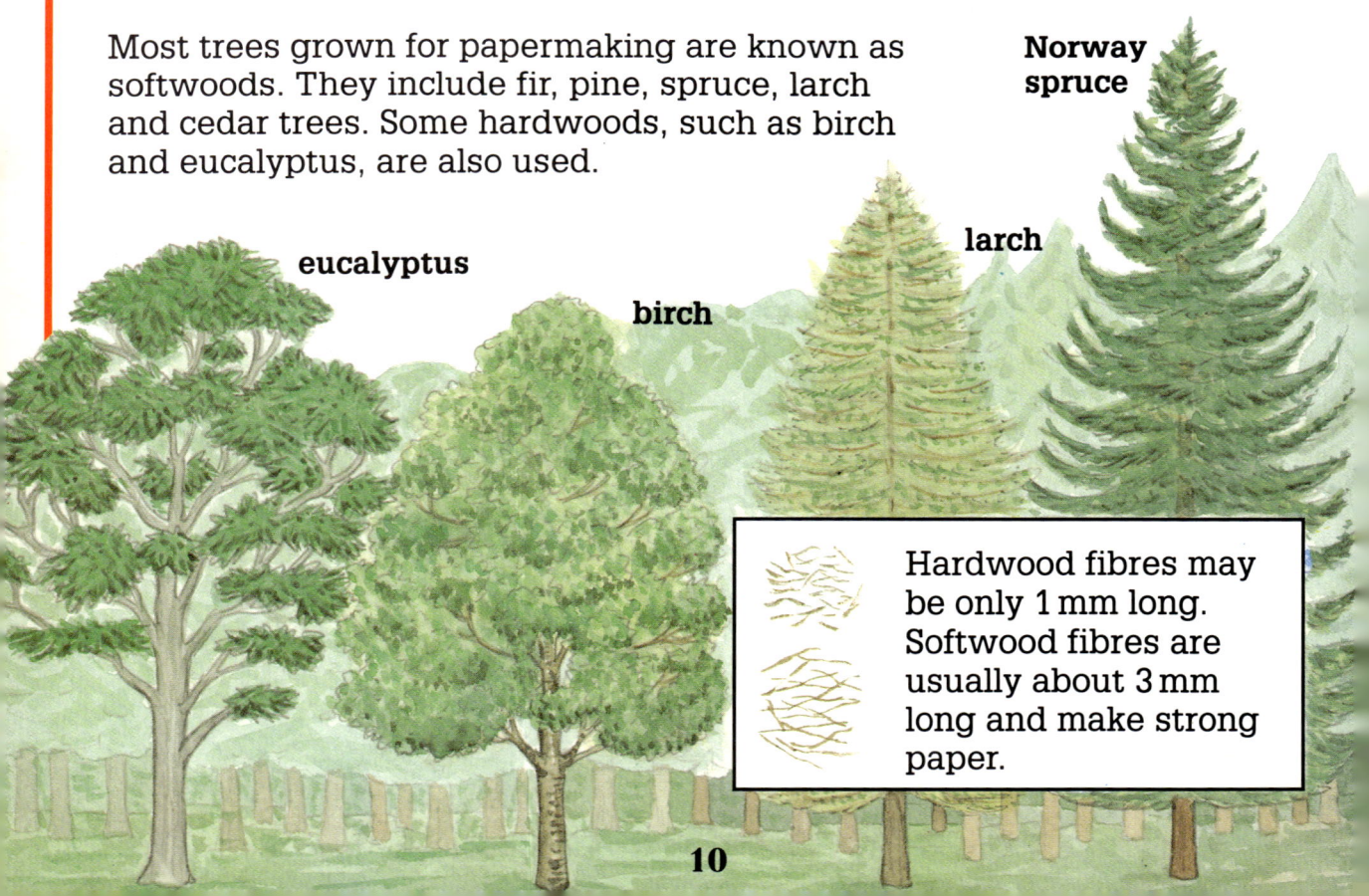

Most trees grown for papermaking are known as softwoods. They include fir, pine, spruce, larch and cedar trees. Some hardwoods, such as birch and eucalyptus, are also used.

eucalyptus

birch

larch

Norway spruce

Hardwood fibres may be only 1 mm long. Softwood fibres are usually about 3 mm long and make strong paper.

It is strange to think of trees as a crop like wheat or potatoes, but they can often be grown in land that is too poor to grow food. Softwood trees are thinned out after about 25 years to give the remaining trees more space and light. When all the trees are felled, new trees are planted.

Sitka spruce

Douglas fir

pine

Try this!

Looking at a piece of paper or a tree, it is hard to believe that they are both made up of lots of tiny fibres, but it *is* possible to see them.

Tear a piece of newspaper and look carefully at the torn edges. The tiny hairs you can see are the cellulose fibres. What do you see if you pull apart a ball of damp tissues?

The ground of a softwood forest is too dark for wildlife to survive. Growing some hardwoods improves the environment.

From tree to timber

If trees are grown for timber for building or making furniture, their trunks need to be thick and straight. But papermakers need the fibres in the wood, not large pieces of timber, so smaller trees can be felled.

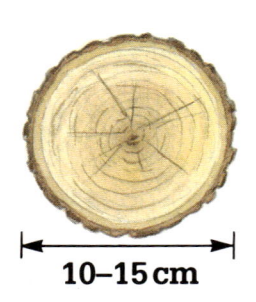

Smaller trees can be ground down into fibres much more quickly. A trunk measuring 10–15 cm across is fine. Some papermakers use the trimmed tops of trees as well.

10–15 cm

To get the fibres needed for paper, the wood has to be ground down at a pulp mill. The first stage is to cut the trunks into logs of a similar size.

Trees grow more slowly in cold climates. In northern Europe, it may be 70 years before a fir tree is ready to be felled. In warmer areas, it may be ready in only 20 years.

Logs are heavy to move. As pulp and paper mills use a lot of water, they are usually near lakes or rivers. An easy way to move the logs is to let them float to the mill!

Try this!

Nearly 12,000 sheets of A4 paper can be made from an average tree. Do you think you use so much paper in a year?

Keep a record of the kinds of paper that your family uses in just one day.

Item	Paper used
Newspapers and magazines	newspaper car mag comic
Stationery	letter to Jo
Cardboard boxes	
Packaging	egg box
Books	
Other	5 paper cups toilet roll

From wood to pulp

To separate the important fibres from other parts of the wood, two ways of making pulp are used.

Mechanical pulp uses almost all the tree. It makes bulky, opaque paper but the sap or lignin it contains will turn yellow in time.

Chemical or woodfree pulp uses only half the tree. The lignin is removed by chemicals. The fibres are longer, making stronger paper.

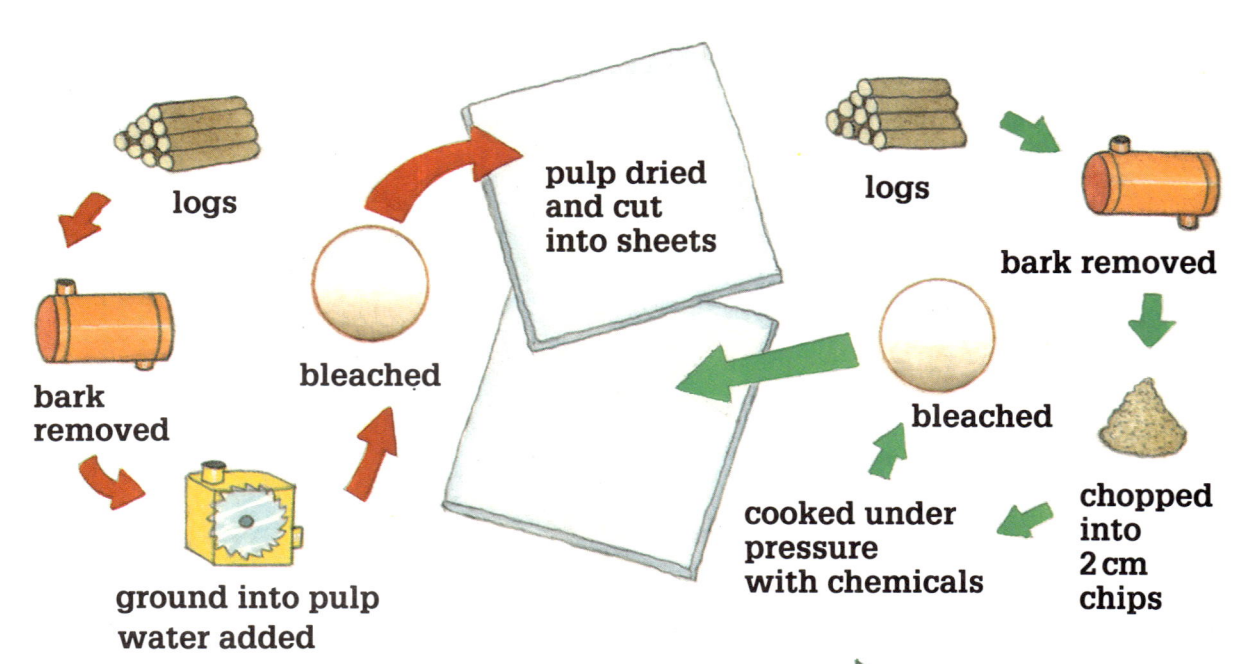

logs → bark removed → ground into pulp water added → bleached → pulp dried and cut into sheets

logs → bark removed → chopped into 2 cm chips → cooked under pressure with chemicals → bleached

When the wood has been pulped, it can be made straight into paper, but often it is dried in thick sheets instead. Bales of these can be sent to a paper mill in another place.

Bark from the logs is not wasted. It may be used as fuel for the pulp mill.

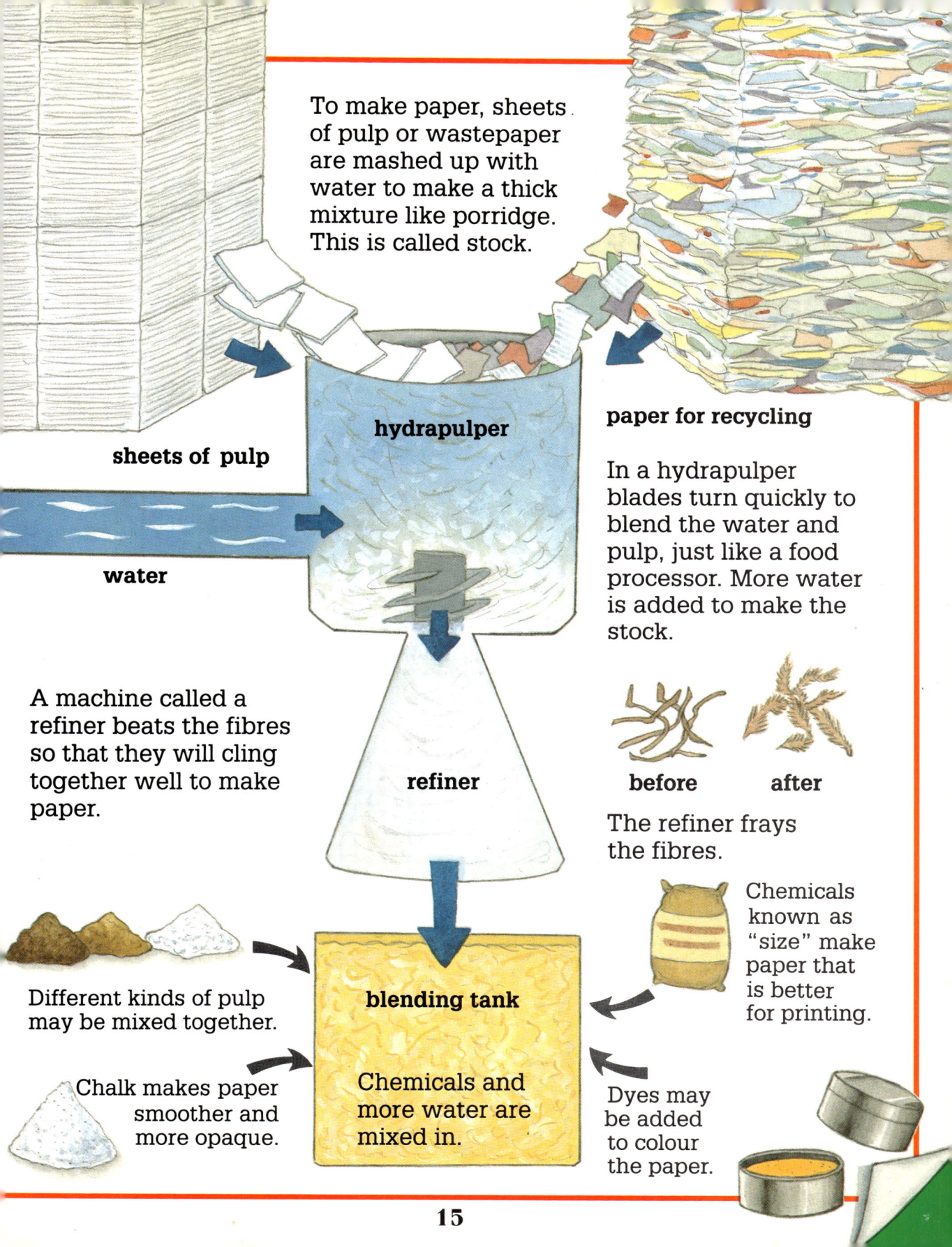

To make paper, sheets of pulp or wastepaper are mashed up with water to make a thick mixture like porridge. This is called stock.

sheets of pulp

water

hydrapulper

paper for recycling

In a hydrapulper blades turn quickly to blend the water and pulp, just like a food processor. More water is added to make the stock.

A machine called a refiner beats the fibres so that they will cling together well to make paper.

refiner

before **after**

The refiner frays the fibres.

Different kinds of pulp may be mixed together.

blending tank

Chemicals and more water are mixed in.

Chalk makes paper smoother and more opaque.

Chemicals known as "size" make paper that is better for printing.

Dyes may be added to colour the paper.

15

From pulp to paper

A papermaking machine may be 100 m long. Stock is poured in at the "wet end" and paper is reeled up at the "dry end".

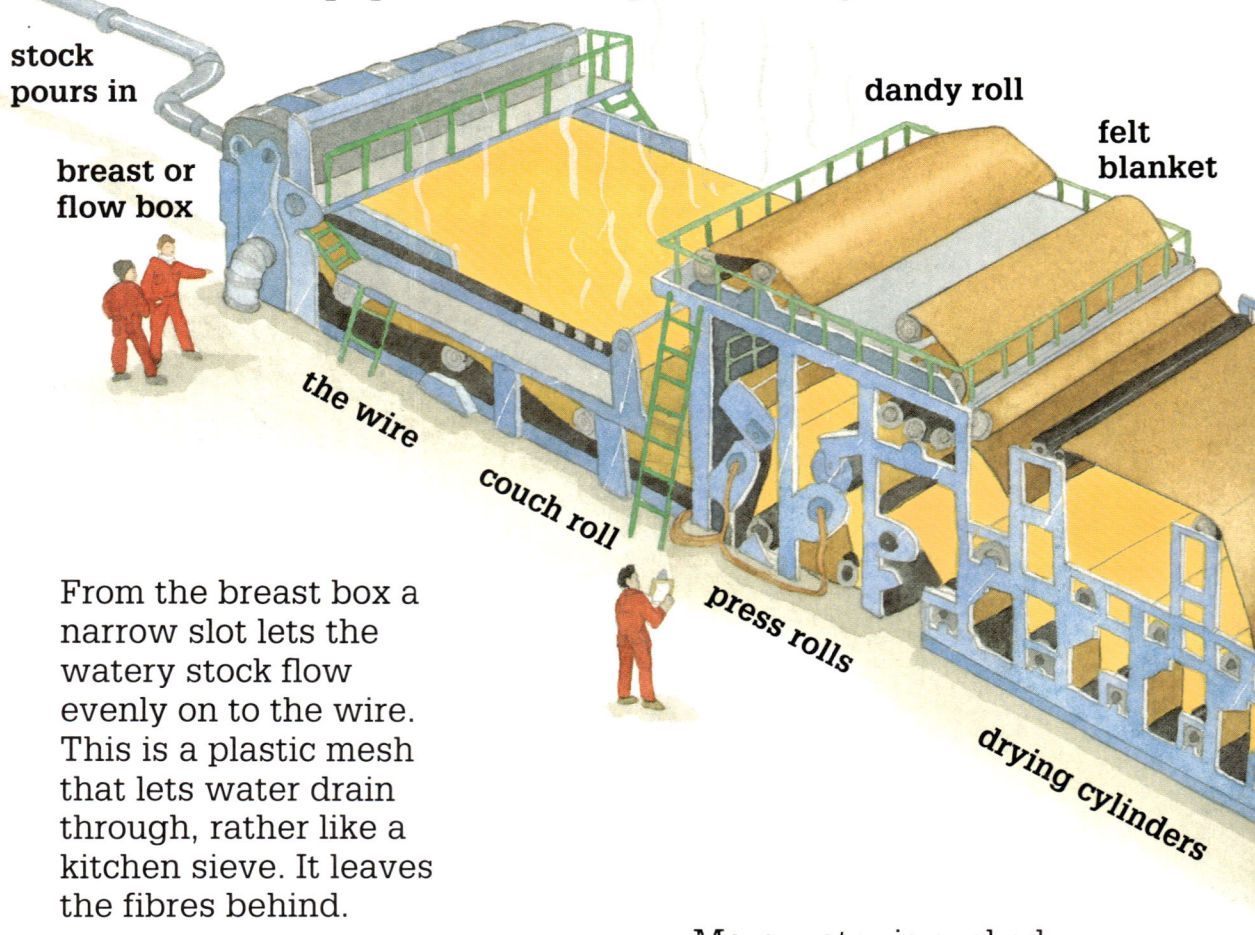

stock pours in

breast or flow box

dandy roll

felt blanket

the wire

couch roll

press rolls

drying cylinders

From the breast box a narrow slot lets the watery stock flow evenly on to the wire. This is a plastic mesh that lets water drain through, rather like a kitchen sieve. It leaves the fibres behind.

More water is sucked out and the fibres form a mat of paper. A felt blanket carries the wet paper through press rolls to squeeze out more water.

🍃 Millions of litres of water are used in papermaking but most is collected and recycled.

Nowadays computers are used to check the paper as it passes through the machine and to control the finished result.

Try this!

Some machines have a dandy roll at the end of the wire. This presses a pattern into the paper called a watermark. You can often see one if you hold writing paper up to the light.

Why not start a collection?

More drying is done by heated cylinders. Size may be applied by the size press. On some machines, after more drying, calender rolls act like an iron to smooth the paper or make it glossy.

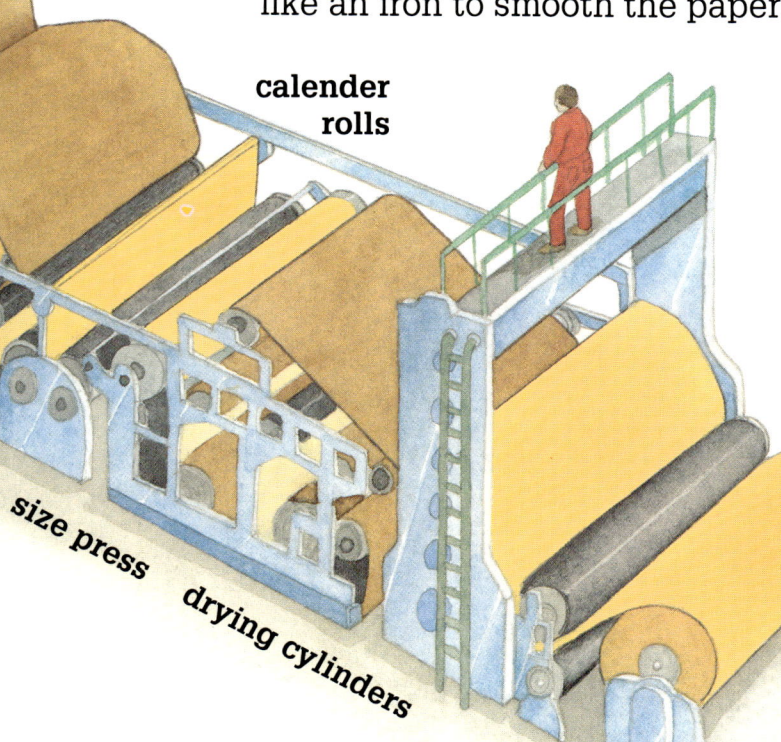

calender rolls

Finally, the paper is wound on to a huge reel holding up to 20 tonnes.

size press

drying cylinders

reel-up

Coating and cutting

Paper from a paper machine feels very smooth and even, but it can be made even more suitable for the job it has to do. Different coatings may be applied to the paper and it can be cut into sheets or smaller reels.

Coating
A coating of china clay can give a glossy surface for printing.

Light-sensitive coating is used on photographic paper. Food can be packed in plastic or wax-coated paper.

Cutting
To cut the large reels of paper into smaller sizes, the paper is unrolled and cut with turning or slicing blades.

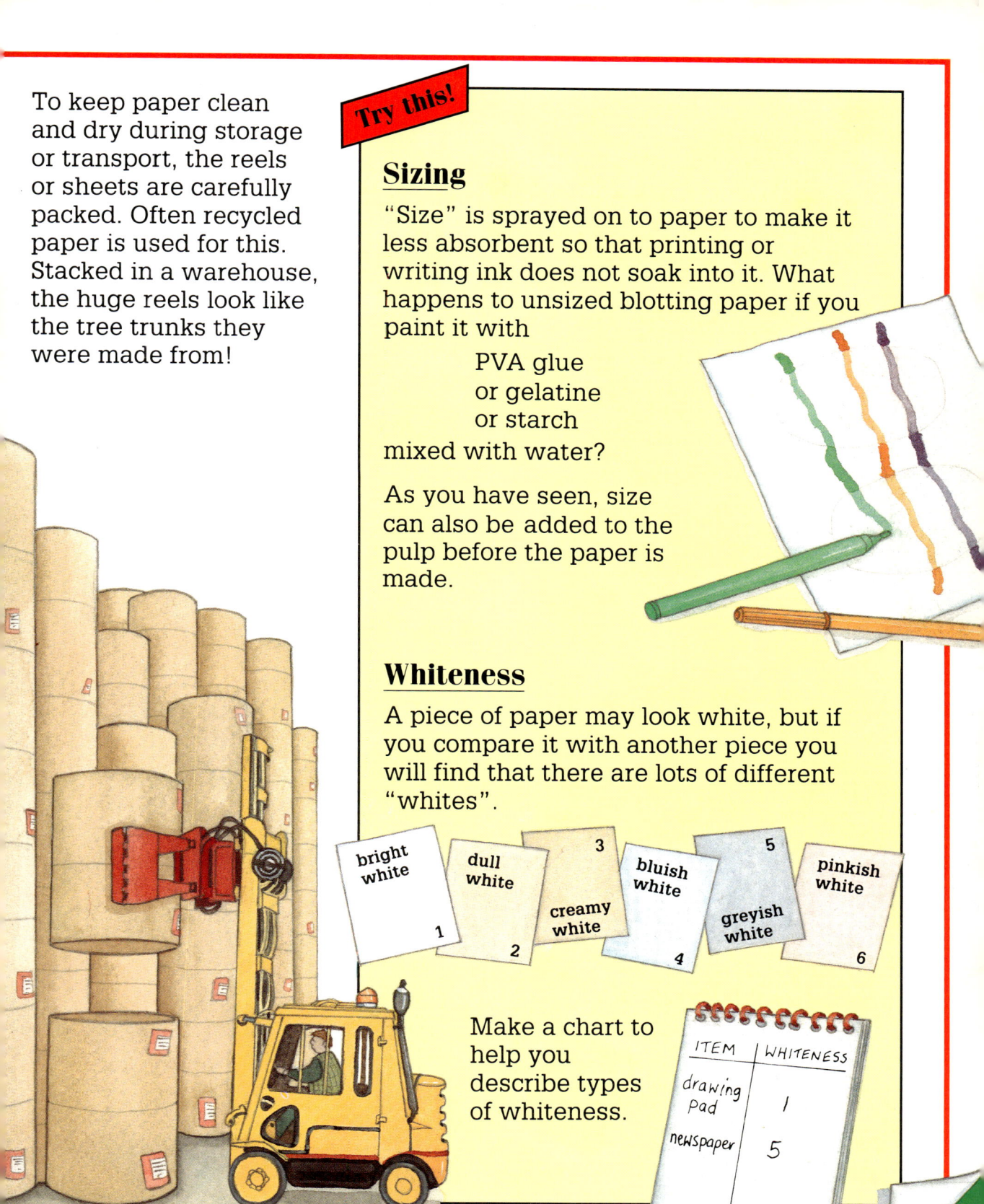

To keep paper clean and dry during storage or transport, the reels or sheets are carefully packed. Often recycled paper is used for this. Stacked in a warehouse, the huge reels look like the tree trunks they were made from!

Try this!

Sizing

"Size" is sprayed on to paper to make it less absorbent so that printing or writing ink does not soak into it. What happens to unsized blotting paper if you paint it with

PVA glue
or gelatine
or starch

mixed with water?

As you have seen, size can also be added to the pulp before the paper is made.

Whiteness

A piece of paper may look white, but if you compare it with another piece you will find that there are lots of different "whites".

1. bright white
2. dull white
3. creamy white
4. bluish white
5. greyish white
6. pinkish white

Make a chart to help you describe types of whiteness.

ITEM	WHITENESS
drawing pad	1
newspaper	5

Looking at paper

There are many different kinds of paper, but all of them are made in a similar way. Whether one kind of paper is suitable for a particular purpose depends on its properties. These tests help to measure some of these properties.

Record your test results in a scrapbook.

Opacity

If paper is opaque, it is hard to see through it.

Draw a thick black line on a piece of card. See how many layers of the paper you are testing have to be laid on the card before you cannot see the black line at all. A low number shows that the paper is very opaque. A high number shows that it is very transparent.

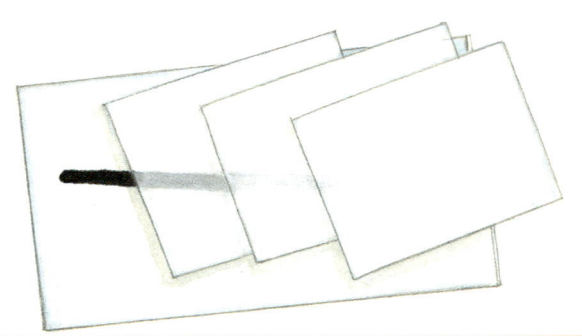

The opposite of opaque is transparent.

You will need:

a piece of white card
a black felt-tip pen

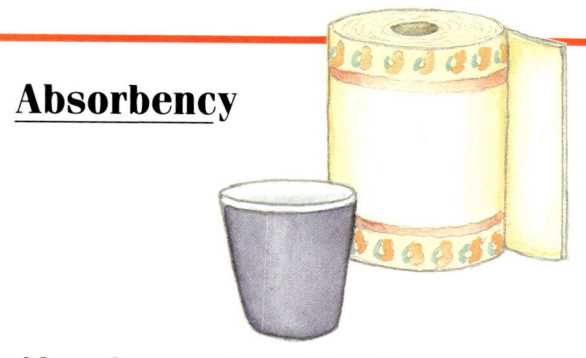

Absorbency

Absorbency describes how well a piece of paper soaks up liquid.

You will need:

a wide-necked jar   scissors
a pot-plant stake   paper clips
coloured water

Cut the pieces of paper for testing into strips and count to ten as you hold them in the water. The one where the colour has spread the furthest is the most absorbent.

coloured water soaks into paper

Strength

Paper carrying heavy weights needs to be strong. Other kinds of paper can be weaker.

You will need:

a pencil and ruler
sand and a spoon
a small bucket

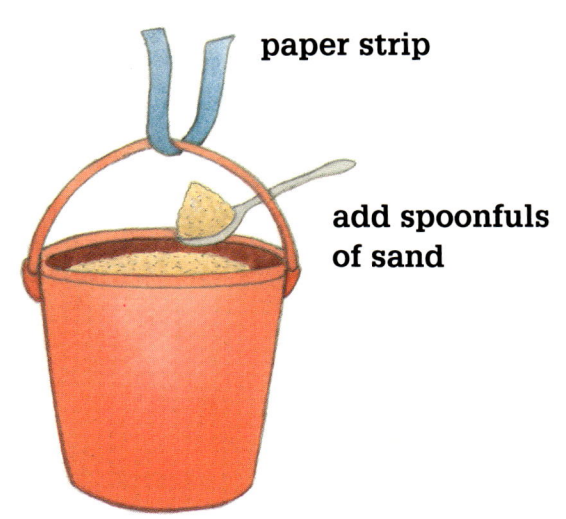

paper strip

add spoonfuls of sand

Cut a strip of the paper you want to test 1 cm wide. Use it to hold a small bucket as in the picture. How many spoonfuls of sand can you add to the bucket before the paper breaks? Test this result against a different type of paper.

Finding the grain

On the wire of a papermaking machine, the fibres tend to line up lengthwise. We call this the grain of the paper. Try to tear a piece of paper in a straight line from the edge. It will tear straighter with the grain than across the grain.

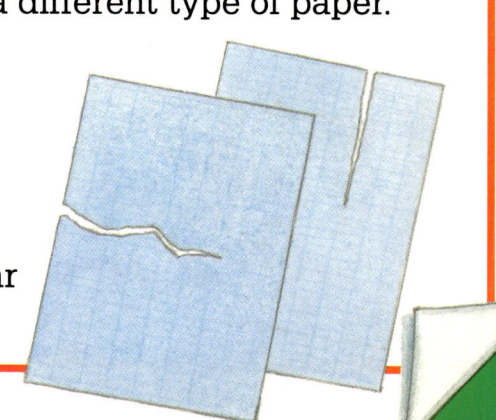

Make your own paper

It is easy and fun to make your own recycled paper. Although your paper will not be as even as machine-made paper, you will be using very similar processes to make it.

You will need:

a wire coathanger
an old pair of tights
scissors
string or elastic band
paper to recycle
2 large buckets
a blender
a large plastic bowl
plenty of water
a blunt knife

1 Soak the paper, torn into small pieces, in water overnight.

← pull open →

tie a knot

tie here

cut here

2 To make your mould, push the coathanger into one leg of the tights and cut and tie as shown above.

3 Blend a little of the soaked paper at a time with plenty of water to make a bucket of pulp.

4 Fill the bowl half full of pulp and dip in your mould as shown.

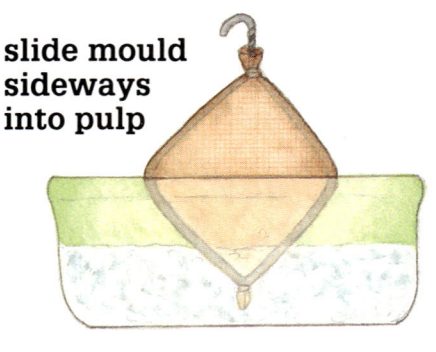

slide mould sideways into pulp

keep mould flat as you push mould down and pull up

5 Let your paper drain, then hang it up to dry. Don't touch it!

leave flat for 5 minutes

hang up to dry

6 After a few hours your paper will feel dry. Lift it carefully with the blunt knife.

knife

lift paper off mould

Try this!

You can use your mould again to make more paper, or you can make more moulds if you want to.

Try adding food colouring or powder paint to your pulp, or try sprinkling pieces of confetti or dried flower petals on your paper at stage 5. But remember that paper needs to be suitable for the job it has to do. Will you want to write on your paper?

Try sizing your paper using the methods on page 19.

Watch out!

- Don't blend your pulp too much! Can you still see tiny fibres?
- Remember to keep your mould flat as you lift it from the pulp.
- Don't drip water on your new, wet paper.

Paper projects

There are hundreds of things that are fun to make with paper, using its different properties.

Papier mâché masks

The absorbency of newspaper means that glue can soak into it. When the glue dries, a hard material is made.

You will need:

old newspapers
wallpaper paste
a balloon
petroleum jelly
scissors
paints and elastic

1 Blow up the balloon and smear petroleum jelly all over it.

2 Stick pieces of torn newspaper dipped in paste over the balloon.

3 When this layer is dry, add another.

Continue until you have a firm covering.

4 Carefully cut the shape in half.

5 Now decorate your masks. You can add papier mâché features and make an elastic fastening.

24

Paper kite

The grain of paper and its crispness mean that it will stay in shape if folded.

You will need:

a large square of paper
sticky tape
strong cotton
ribbon or paper streamer

1 Fold the paper in half diagonally and open it out again.

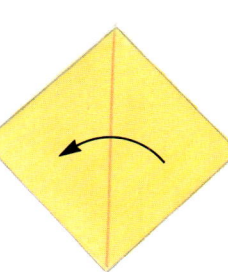

2 Fold the sides to the middle.

3 Fold up the edges as shown.

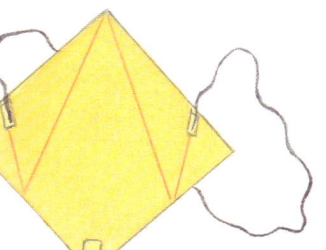

4 Open and stick on cotton "strings" and a streamer.

Palm tree

Turn newspapers back into trees like the one in the picture!

You will need:
newspapers   paints
stapler   sticky tape
scissors

1 Roll newspapers into tubes and staple them into rings.

2 Push one ring into another to make a trunk.

3 Cut the ends of rolls of newspaper to make leaves.

cut along lines

4 Push the leaves into the top. Paint your tree.

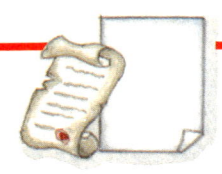

Paper past...

◆ Paper was invented in China nearly 2,000 years ago. It was made of pulped rags and fishing nets drained on a bamboo sieve.

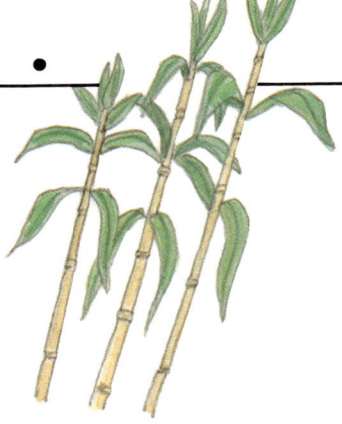

◆ The word "paper" comes from ancient Egyptian papyrus. But papyrus is made from flattened reeds – it isn't really paper at all!

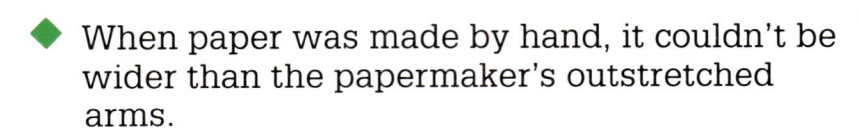

◆ When paper was made by hand, it couldn't be wider than the papermaker's outstretched arms.

◆ Until the last century, most paper was made from old rags beaten into pulp. Cotton and linen are made from plants so they are a good source of cellulose fibres.

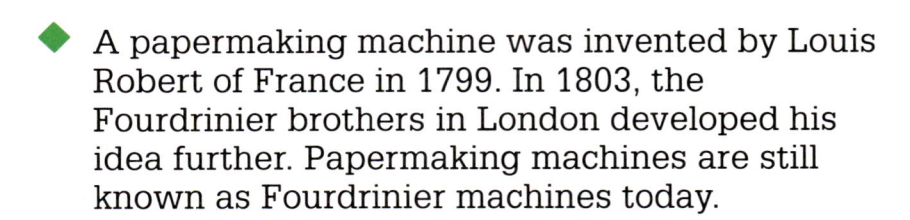

◆ A papermaking machine was invented by Louis Robert of France in 1799. In 1803, the Fourdrinier brothers in London developed his idea further. Papermaking machines are still known as Fourdrinier machines today.

. . . and present

◆ Banknotes are still made using cotton fibres because they are very strong.

◆ It takes nearly 60,000 litres of water to make one tonne of paper.

◆ When scientists realised that wood would be a good source of cellulose fibre, they were copying wasps! Many wasps chew the bark of trees to make paper nests.

◆ At the wet end of a paper machine the paper is 99% water – at the dry end it is only 6% water.

◆ Rainforests are not cut down to make paper. They are cleared for other reasons – the wood is not suitable for making paper anyway.

◆ Paper on a paper machine travels at up to 120 kilometres per hour.

Glossary

Absorbency
This describes how much liquid paper can soak up.

Calender roll
A roller that smooths and polishes paper passing over it.

Cellulose
A substance found in plants.

China clay
A fine powder used to coat paper to make the surface smooth and opaque.

Couch roll
A roller on to which the paper in a paper machine is carried when it is strong enough to support itself.

Dandy roll
A light roller made of wire that presses a pattern on paper at the wet end of a paper machine.

Fibre
A hair-like strand of material such as cellulose.

Grain
The direction that most of the fibres lie in a sheet of paper.

Hardwood
Wood from trees such as birch or oak that lose their leaves in winter.

Hydrapulper
A tank in which blades mash bales of pulp or wastepaper and water into a porridge-like mixture.

Lignin
A material that sticks together the cellulose fibres in wood. If left in pulp, it gradually turns paper yellow.

Opacity
This describes how see-through paper is.

Paper
A material made of cellulose fibres matted together to form a sheet.

Press rolls
Rollers that paper passes between in a paper machine to squeeze out water.

Refiner
A cone-shaped drum in which fibres are beaten before passing into the paper machine.

Size
Chemicals added to the stock or the surface of paper to make it less absorbent.

Softwood
Wood from cone-bearing or coniferous trees such as fir or pine.

Stock
The mixture of pulp and water that is fed into a paper machine.

Watermark
A mark pressed into paper by a dandy roll.

Wire
The moving plastic mesh where paper is first formed in a paper machine.

Index

absorbency 21, 24, 28

bank notes 27
bark 14, 27
birch 10, 28
bleach 4
blending tank 15
blotting paper 19
books 13
breast box 16

calender rolls 17, 28
cardboard 8, 13
cedar 10
cellulose 10, 11, 26, 27, 28
chalk 15
China 26
china clay 18, 28
climate 13
coatings 18
computers 17
couch roll 16, 28
cutting 18

dandy roll 17, 28
dry end 16, 27
drying cylinders 16, 17
dyes 15, 23

environment 11
eucalyptus 10
Europe 13

felling trees 11, 12, 13
felt blanket 16
fibres 10, 11, 12, 14, 15, 16, 21, 26, 27, 28
fir 10, 11, 13, 28
flow box 16
forests 10

grain 21, 25, 28

hardwoods 10, 11, 28
hydrapulper 15, 28

ink 19

kites 25

larch 10
light-sensitive coating 18
lignin 14, 28
logs 12, 13, 14

magazines 13
masks 24
mould 22, 23

newspaper 11, 13, 19, 24, 25

oak 28
opacity 14, 15, 20, 28

packaging 13, 18, 19
paper machine 16, 17, 18, 26, 27, 28
paper mill 13, 14
papier mâché 24
papyrus 26
photographic paper 18
pine 10, 11, 28
planting trees 11
plastic-coated paper 18
press rolls 16, 28
printing 15, 18, 19
pulp 12, 13, 14, 15, 16, 26, 28
pulp mill 13, 14

rags 26
rainforests 27
recycled paper 15, 19, 22, 23
reels 16, 17, 18, 19
refiner 15, 28

sap 14
scrapbook 20
sheets 18
size 15, 17, 19, 23, 28
size press 17
softwoods 10, 11, 28
spruce 10, 11
stationery 13
stock 15, 16, 28
storage 19
strength 21

timber 12
tissues 8, 11
transparency 20
transport 19
trees 10, 11, 12, 13, 14, 25
tree trunks 12, 19

warehouse 19
wastepaper 15, 20
water 13, 14, 15, 16, 17, 27, 28
watermark 17, 28
wax-coated paper 18
wet end 16, 27, 28
whiteness 19
wildlife 11
wire 16, 17, 21, 28
wood 12, 14, 17, 28
writing paper 17

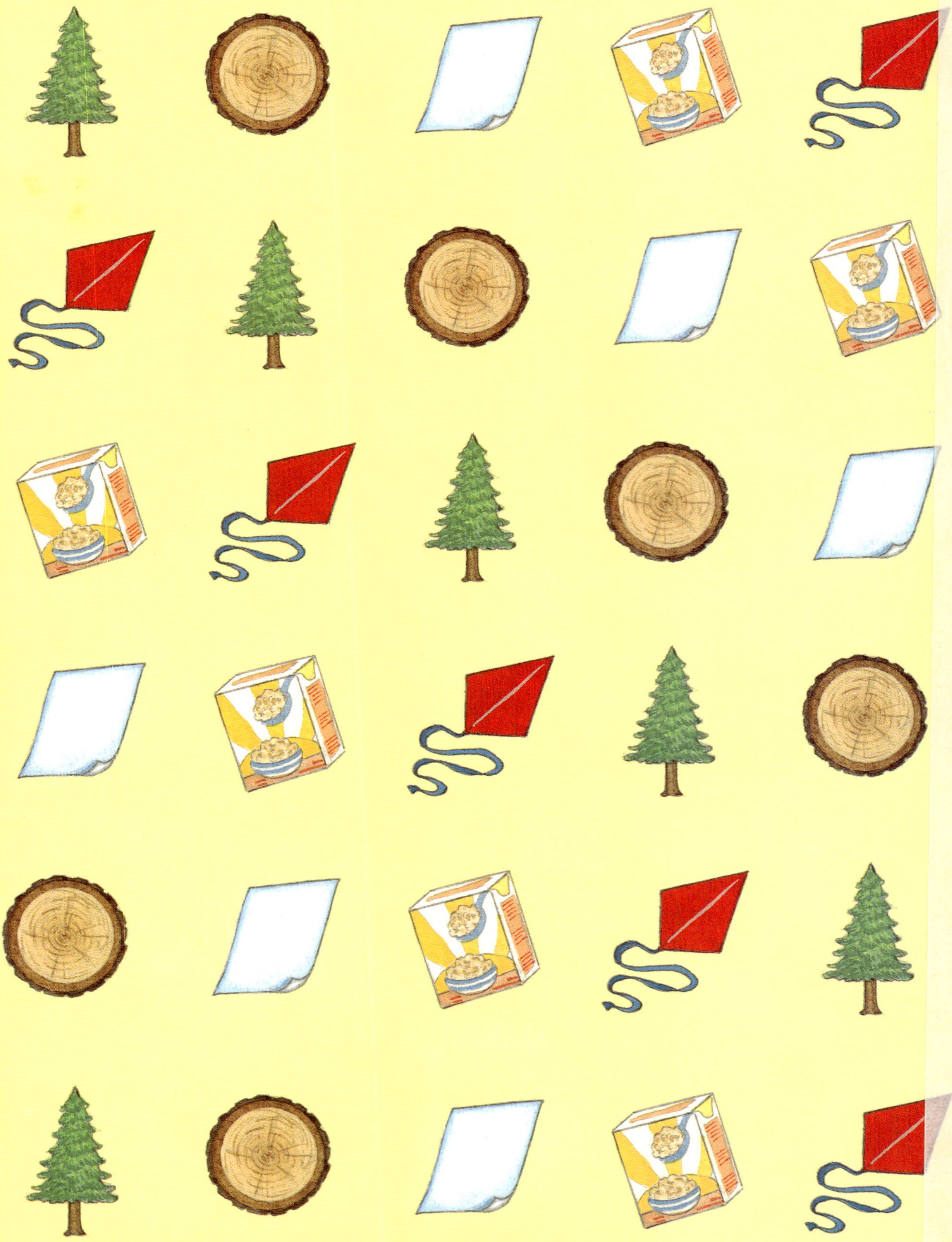